ARROW BOOK OF

Easy
Cooking

(Let's Cook Without Cooking)

By ESTHER RUDOMIN

Illustrated by LEE SMITH

SCHOLASTIC  BOOK SERVICES

Published by Scholastic Book Services, a division
of Scholastic Magazines, Inc., New York, N.Y.

CONTENTS

Copyright 1955 by Esther Rudomin. Copyright © 1962 by Scholastic Magazines, Inc. This edition is published by Scholastic Book Services, a division of Scholastic Magazines, Inc., by arrangement with Thomas Y. Crowell Company.

5th printing . . . . November 1966
Printed in the U.S.A.

General Directions

Good cooks always follow these simple rules when working with food:

1. Read each recipe through to the end very carefully, to be sure that you have all the ingredients for it and to see how long it takes to prepare. Some dishes can be eaten as soon as they are ready, but others must be put in the refrigerator for an hour or more, and some even overnight.

2. When you shop for food needed for the recipe, be sure to check the weights given on the cans, frozen food packages, and jars, to see that they are correct for your dish.

3. Before starting a recipe, wash your hands very, very carefully and put on an apron. If your hair is long and worn loosely, tie it up with a ribbon so that none of it gets into the food.

4. Follow the directions given for each recipe. Be exact in measuring ingredients. Don't ever use more or less than the recipe calls for.

5. Be careful when using sharp knives, can openers, or food graters. It's better to be slow in preparing a dish than to hurry and then be sorry!

6. Put on the table all the equipment and food you will need. If you can, work on the counter space near the sink, rather than on the table. There will be less chance of spilling things on the floor if you are near the sink.

7. Clean up as you go along. As you finish using one utensil put it right into the sink. Don't let it stand around on the table or counter and clutter up your working space. Throw away all rubbish immediately.

8. As soon as you have finished preparing a dish, wash and dry all the utensils you've used, and put them away where you found them. Wipe the table or counter space and sweep the floor, so that the kitchen looks neat and tidy.

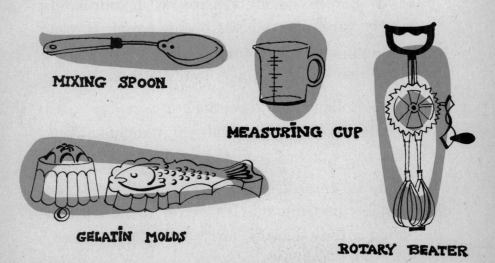

MIXING SPOON

MEASURING CUP

GELATIN MOLDS

ROTARY BEATER

9. When serving salads, juices, and cakes, use paper plates and cups whenever possible. They will save a lot of dishwashing after the meal!

10. Be sure that what you serve not only tastes good, but looks nice. It is very important to have a pretty table and an attractively served meal. You can buy inexpensive paper place mats, tablecloths, and napkins to brighten up a table. Paper doilies can be used often as the recipes in this book will show you.

That's about it. Remember, read the recipes through, follow the directions, be neat and careful, and you will be a grade A cook.

NOW GO AHEAD — COOK WITHOUT COOKING, AND HAVE FUN!

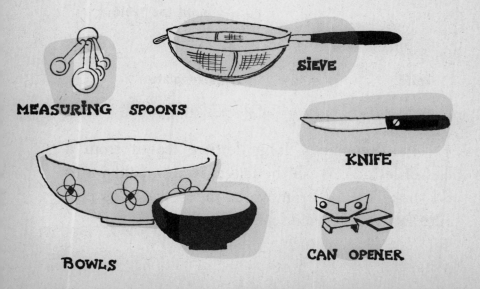

MEASURING SPOONS

SIEVE

KNIFE

BOWLS

CAN OPENER

Appetizers

Antipasto

(FOR 4 PEOPLE)

You will need:

4 large lettuce leaves	2 large tomatoes
4 Gruyère cheese triangles	1 cucumber
4 thin slices Italian salami or plain Bologna	4 stalks celery
	Oil and vinegar to pass around the table

You will use:

1 knife	4 salad plates

Prepare it this way:

1. Remove 4 large lettuce leaves from a head of lettuce. Wash the leaves well in cold water and shake them to remove as much water as possible. Put one lettuce leaf on each plate.

2. Take the paper off the 4 Gruyère cheese triangles and put one triangle on each of the four plates, beside the lettuce.

3. Put one slice of salami or Bologna on each lettuce leaf.

4. Wash the tomatoes and celery in cold water and dry. Peel the cucumber.

5. Cut the 2 tomatoes into quarters, so that you can put 2 pieces of tomato on each lettuce leaf.

6. Cut the leaves from the 4 stalks of celery and put one stalk on each plate.

7. Cut the peeled cucumber into thin slices and divide the slices into 4 portions. Arrange one portion of cucumber slices on each lettuce leaf.

8. Pass the vinegar and oil around the table and you will be ready to eat this Italian appetizer. It's good.

Summer Fruit Cup

(FOR 4 PEOPLE)

You will need:

2 packages frozen melon balls

1 8-ounce can pitted cherries

¼ cup dry ginger ale

¼ cup diluted frozen orange juice

You will use:

Mixing bowl

Can opener

Sieve

1 large bowl to use with the sieve

1 large plate or aluminum foil

Measuring cup

Mixing spoon

4 small bowls

8

Prepare it this way:

1. Put the melon balls into the mixing bowl and let defrost on the kitchen table for about 2 hours.

2. Open the can of cherries and place the cherries in a sieve over the other bowl to drain. You will not use the cherry syrup. When the cherries are well drained, add them to the melon balls in the mixing bowl.

3. Cover the bowl with a plate or aluminum foil and put into the refrigerator for at least 1 hour.

4. Just before serving, measure ¼ cup ginger ale and ¼ cup diluted frozen orange juice and add them to the fruit.

5. Mix a little with the spoon and put the melon balls and cherries into the 4 small fruit bowls.

6. With a spoon, pour a little of the ginger ale and orange juice from the bowl over the fruit in each dish.

Tomato Sour Cream Soup

(FOR 4 PEOPLE)

You will need:

2 10½-ounce cans tomato soup

1 cup sour cream

1 cup cold water

½ cucumber

16 salty crackers

You will use:

Can opener

1 big bowl

Measuring cup

1 big spoon

1 large plate or aluminum foil

1 knife

4 soup plates

Prepare it this way:

1. Open both cans of soup and pour the soup into the bowl.

2. Measure 1 cup sour cream and add it to the soup. Stir slowly until the sour cream is well mixed with the soup.

3. Add 1 cup cold water slowly to the soup and sour cream, stirring until it is all mixed together.

4. Cover the bowl with a plate or aluminum foil and put into the refrigerator for at least 1 hour.

5. Just before serving, peel ½ cucumber. Cut the cucumber into thin slices and add to the soup.

6. Pour the soup into the soup plates and serve with salty crackers.

Cold Clam Bisque

(FOR 4 PEOPLE)

You will need:

1 10½-ounce can
cream of tomato soup

1 10½-ounce can
cream of mushroom
soup

1 10-ounce can
minced clams

2 cups milk

You will use:

Can opener

1 big bowl

Measuring cup

Rotary beater

1 mixing spoon

1 large plate or
aluminum foil

4 soup plates

Prepare it this way:

1. Open the cans of cream of tomato and cream of mushroom soup and minced clams. Pour the soups and the minced clams, together with the clam juice, into the big bowl.

2. Add a little of the 2 cups milk slowly, then beat with the rotary beater. Add a little more milk and beat again. Do this until all the milk is used.

3. Cover the bowl with a plate or with aluminum foil.

4. Chill in the refrigerator for at least 2 hours, and then pour into the soup plates and serve. This soup is a meal in itself.

Chilled Cream of Chicken Soup

(FOR 4 PEOPLE)

You will need:

1 10½-ounce can cream of chicken soup	¼ teaspoon salt
1 8-ounce jar or can applesauce	¼ teaspoon white pepper
1½ cups milk	¼ teaspoon curry powder

You will use:

Can opener	Rotary beater
1 big bowl	Measuring spoons
Sieve	1 large plate or aluminum foil
Mixing spoon	4 soup plates
Measuring cup	

Prepare it this way:

1. Open the can of cream of chicken soup. Put the sieve over the bowl and put the soup into the sieve.

2. Open the jar or can of applesauce and add it to the soup in the sieve.

1.   2.

3. With the mixing spoon, stir the soup and applesauce mixture in the sieve until it all goes through into the bowl. You will have a few pieces of chicken left in the sieve; throw them out.

4. Very slowly, add a little of the 1½ cups milk to the soup and applesauce mixture. Mix it in with the rotary beater. Then add a little more milk and beat again. Do this until you have added all the milk and the soup looks nice and smooth.

5. Add ¼ teaspoon salt, ¼ teaspoon white pepper, and ¼ teaspoon of curry powder and mix well with the spoon.

6. Cover the bowl with a plate or aluminum foil and put it into the refrigerator for at least 2 hours. When the soup is very cold, pour it into the soup plates and serve. Pass around salt and pepper, in case your family or friends like their soup to be more spicy.

Salads

Cream Cheese Salad Dressing

You will need:

1 3-ounce package
cream cheese

1 teaspoon
confectioners' sugar

1 teaspoon diluted
frozen lemon juice

1 cup ready-made
French dressing

You will use:

Mixing bowl
and spoon

Measuring cup
and spoon

Pitcher

Prepare it this way:

Put the cream cheese into the mixing bowl. Add the sugar and the lemon juice and mix well. Slowly add 1 cup French dressing. Stir well. Pour the mixture into the pitcher and chill 1 hour before serving.

Chicken-Apple Salad
(FOR 4 PEOPLE)

You will need:

2 5-ounce cans boned chicken

3 stalks celery (without leaves)

2 red unpeeled apples

1 cup fresh seedless grapes

2 tablespoons diluted frozen lemon juice

½ cup mayonnaise

4 large lettuce leaves

You will use:

Can opener

Sieve

Mixing bowl

1 knife

Measuring cup

Measuring spoon

Mixing spoon

1 large plate or aluminum foil

4 paper plates

Prepare it this way:

1. Open the two 5-ounce cans boned chicken. Put the sieve over a bowl. Then put the chicken into the sieve to let all the broth drain off.

2. After 5 minutes, throw away the broth that has drained off the chicken. Take the chicken out of the sieve and put it in the mixing bowl.

3. Cut the celery stalks to make 1 cupful. Add the chopped celery to the chicken in the bowl.

4. Wash and dry the 2 red apples. Do not peel them. Cut out the cores and chop the apples into pieces about one inch big. Put the apple chunks into the bowl with the chicken and the celery.

5. Pour the 2 tablespoons lemon juice over the apples in the bowl.

6. Cut the seedless grapes in half and put them into the bowl.

7. Mix the chicken, celery, apples, and grapes all together.

8. Add ½ cup mayonnaise and stir the salad well. Cover the bowl with a plate or aluminum foil and put it into the refrigerator for at least 1 hour before serving.

9. Wash and dry the 4 large lettuce leaves.

10. Put one lettuce leaf on each of the paper plates. Pile the salad on top of each leaf and serve.

Corned Beef and Potato Salad

(FOR 4 PEOPLE)

You will need:

1 1-pound can potatoes

3 stalks celery (without leaves)

⅓ cup mayonnaise

1 tablespoon vinegar

½ teaspoon salt

¼ teaspoon pepper

1 12-ounce can corned beef

You will use:

Can opener

Sieve

1 large bowl for the sieve

1 knife

1 mixing bowl

Measuring cup

Measuring spoons

Mixing spoon

4 plates

Prepare it this way:

1. Place the sieve over the large bowl.

2. Open the can of potatoes and put the potatoes into the sieve to drain off the water.

3. Cut the potatoes into small-sized pieces and put them into the mixing bowl.

20

4. Cut up the celery stalks into tiny pieces and add the pieces to the potatoes in the mixing bowl.

5. Add ⅓ cup mayonnaise, 1 tablespoon vinegar, ½ teaspoon salt, and ¼ teaspoon pepper. Mix well with the potatoes and celery.

6. Open the can of corned beef and cut the beef into medium-sized pieces.

7. Add the beef to the bowl with the potatoes, celery, and mayonnaise. Mix a little. Put the bowl on the table and let everyone help himself.

Tuna Fish Salad

(FOR 4 PEOPLE)

You will need:

1 7-ounce can tuna fish

4 stalks celery (without leaves)

1 cucumber

1 tablespoon diluted frozen lemon juice

4 medium-sized tomatoes

¼ cup mayonnaise

¼ teaspoon salt

¼ teaspoon pepper

4 lettuce leaves

You will use:

Can opener

1 big mixing bowl

Knife

Measuring cup

Measuring spoons

Mixing spoon

1 large plate or aluminum foil

4 paper plates

Prepare it this way:

1. Open the can of tuna fish with the can opener and put the tuna, together with the oil, into the mixing bowl.

2. Cut up the celery into tiny pieces. (You have, of course, washed the celery.) Add the celery to the tuna fish.

22

3. Peel the cucumber and cut it into tiny pieces. Add the cucumber to the celery and the tuna fish.

4. Measure ¼ cup mayonnaise, 1 tablespoon lemon juice, ¼ teaspoon salt, and ¼ teaspoon pepper. Add these to the tuna fish, celery, and cucumber mixture. Mix with a spoon so that the tuna fish is well broken up. Cover the bowl with a large plate or aluminum foil and put into the refrigerator for at least 2 hours.

5. When you are ready to serve the salad, wash and dry the tomatoes. Cut each tomato almost through into 6 parts and arrange it like a flower.

6. Wash and dry the lettuce leaves. Put each one on a paper plate and place a tomato flower in the center of each lettuce leaf. Put the tuna fish salad into the tomato flower. You will have four very filling salads, and they will look very pretty.

Ham Rolls with Carrot Sticks

(FOR 4 PEOPLE)

You will need:

- ¼ pound cream cheese
- 2 tablespoons light cream or evaporated milk
- 12 stuffed olives
- ¼ teaspoon salt
- ¼ teaspoon pepper
- 4 large slices boiled ham
- 4 carrots

You will use:

- Mixing bowl
- Measuring spoons
- Mixing spoon
- Knife
- Wooden bread board
- 4 toothpicks
- 1 large plate
- Wax paper
- 4 paper plates

Prepare it this way:

1. Put the cream cheese into the mixing bowl. Add to it 2 tablespoons light cream or evaporated milk and mix very well, so that the cheese is smooth.

2. Chop 12 stuffed olives very fine and add them to the cheese. Then add ¼ teaspoon salt and ¼ teaspoon pepper. Mix it all together with the spoon.

24

3. Put the ham slices on the board and spread each one with some of the cheese and olive mixture. Roll each slice of ham and fasten it with a toothpick. Carefully place the ham rolls on a plate and put them into the refrigerator to chill for at least 1 hour.

4. Just before serving, wash and dry 4 lettuce leaves and put one on each of the paper plates. Place one ham roll on each lettuce leaf.

5. Scrape the 4 carrots with the knife until they are clean and rinse them with cold water. Cut each carrot into 8 long sticks. Place 8 carrot sticks on each plate with the ham roll. The soft ham and the crunchy carrots will go well together.

Tomato Vegetable Salad

(FOR 4 PEOPLE)

You will need:

4 large solid
  tomatoes

2 8-ounce cans
  mixed vegetables

1 tablespoon
  mayonnaise

¼ teaspoon salt

¼ teaspoon pepper

4 lettuce leaves

Hard seeded rolls
  and butter

You will use:

Knife

1 teaspoon

Glass jar

Can opener

Sieve

1 large bowl to use
  with the sieve

Mixing bowl

Measuring spoons

Mixing spoon

4 paper plates

Prepare it this way:

1. Cut a slice from the top of each of the 4 tomatoes. Scoop out the insides, or pulp, of the tomatoes with the teaspoon. Be careful not to go through the skins of the tomatoes. Put the pulp in a glass jar and put the jar in the refrigerator. You won't need the insides of the tomatoes for this salad, but your mother may be able to use them some other time.

2. Open the 2 cans of mixed vegetables. Put the vegetables into the sieve over the large bowl to drain off the water. After the vegetables are drained, put them into the mixing bowl.

3. Add 1 tablespoon mayonnaise, ¼ teaspoon salt, and ¼ teaspoon pepper. Mix with the spoon, then carefully put the vegetables into the tomato cups you have made. Put the tomato cups into the refrigerator for at least 2 hours before serving.

4. Just before serving, wash and dry the 4 lettuce leaves and put one on each plate. Put a tomato cup on top of each lettuce leaf. Serve with hard rolls and butter.

Salmon Salad

You will need:

1 7¾-ounce can salmon

1 8¼-ounce can green peas

4 stalks celery (without leaves)

¼ cup mayonnaise

¼ teaspoon white pepper

¼ teaspoon salt

1 green pepper

4 lettuce leaves

You will use:

Can opener

Mixing bowl

Sieve

1 large bowl to use with the sieve

Knife

Measuring cup

Measuring spoons

Mixing spoon

4 paper plates

Prepare it this way:

1. Open the can of salmon. Put the salmon, together with the oil, into the mixing bowl.

2. Open the can of peas. Put the peas in the sieve over the large bowl to drain off the water. After the peas are drained, add them to the salmon.

3. Wash the 4 stalks celery and cut them into small pieces. Add the celery to the salmon and the peas.

4. Measure ¼ cup mayonnaise, ¼ teaspoon salt, and ¼ teaspoon white pepper. Add them to the salmon mixture in the bowl. Mix with the spoon so that the salmon is broken apart and well mixed with the peas and the celery. Put into the refrigerator for at least 2 hours.

5. When you are ready to serve the salad, wash and dry the green pepper. Cut a slice from the top, cut out the core, and remove all the seeds. Slice the pepper crosswise into 4 rings.

6. Wash and dry the 4 lettuce leaves and put one in the center of each plate. Place the pepper rings over them.

7. Place a portion of the salmon salad over the pepper rings and serve.

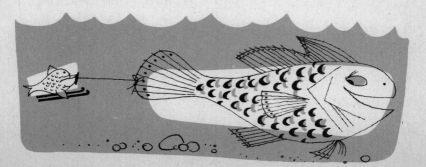

Jellied Waldorf Salad

(FOR 4 PEOPLE)

You will need:

- 1 package orange gelatin
- 2 cups hot water from the tap
- 1 tablespoon vinegar
- ¼ teaspoon salt
- 3 apples
- ½ cup canned chopped walnuts
- 2 celery stalks (without leaves)
- 4 lettuce leaves
- Cream Cheese Dressing (for recipe see page 16)

You will use:

- Mixing bowl
- Measuring cup
- Mixing spoon
- Measuring spoons
- Knife
- Salad mold
- 4 paper plates

Prepare it this way:

1. Open 1 package orange gelatin and put the gelatin powder into the bowl. Add 2 cups hot water from the tap and stir until the gelatin dissolves. Add 1 tablespoon vinegar and mix it into the gelatin.

30

2. Wash the apples and cut out the cores, but do not peel them. Cut the apples into very small pieces and add them to the gelatin.

3. Cut up the celery into little pieces and put it into the gelatin. Add ½ cup chopped walnuts. Mix them all together with the gelatin.

4. Put the gelatin mixture into the mold and let it stand in the refrigerator for at least 6 hours.

5. Just before serving, unmold the gelatin by dipping the mold for ½ minute—not longer—into a bowl of warm water, so that the water covers the bottom and comes halfway up the sides of the mold. Then turn the mold over on a plate.

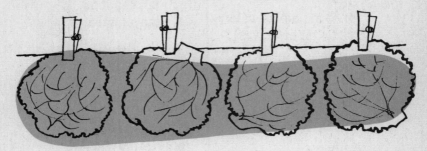

6. Wash and dry the 4 lettuce leaves. Put one leaf on each plate and place a portion of the jellied salad on each leaf. Pass the Cream Cheese Dressing around the table.

Macaroni and Bologna Salad

(FOR 4 PEOPLE)

You will need:

1 16-ounce can macaroni in cheese sauce	14 stuffed olives
	4 lettuce leaves
1 medium-sized green pepper	12 slices (about ¾ pound) bologna
2 large stalks celery (without leaves)	2 tablespoons mayonnaise

You will use:

Can opener	Mixing spoon
Mixing bowl	4 paper plates
Knife	Measuring spoon

Prepare it this way:

1. Open the can of macaroni and put it into the mixing bowl.

2. Wash and dry 1 medium-sized green pepper. Cut it open and take out the core and all the little seeds. Cut into little pieces. Add the green pepper bits to the macaroni in the bowl.

3. Wash and cut the celery stalks into small pieces. Add the celery to the macaroni and green pepper in the bowl.

4. Cut 10 of the stuffed olives into little pieces and add them to the bowl with the macaroni, pepper, and celery. Mix a little with the spoon.

5. Wash and dry 4 lettuce leaves.

6. Put 1 lettuce leaf on each of the 4 paper plates. Then place 1 slice bologna in the center of each leaf. On top of the bologna slices, put some of the macaroni salad. Cover the macaroni salad with another slice of bologna. On top of the second slice of bologna on each side of the four plates put more of the macaroni salad. Top each serving with 1 more slice of bologna. You will have a triple-decker salad. Spread the top slice of bologna on each plate with ½ tablespoon mayonnaise and place 1 whole olive in the center.

Pear Beauty Salad

(FOR 4 PEOPLE)

You will need:

8 canned pear halves

1 8-ounce package cream cheese

2 tablespoons light cream or evaporated milk

4 lettuce leaves

60 large fresh Bing cherries or Tokay grapes

Bottled French dressing

You will use:

Can opener

Sieve

1 large bowl to use with the sieve

Mixing bowl

Measuring spoon

Mixing spoon

Spatula

1 small knife

4 paper plates

Prepare it this way:

1. Open the can of pear halves. With a spoon, take out 8 pear halves and put them into the sieve over the large bowl to drain.

2. While the pears are draining, put the package of cream cheese into the mixing bowl and add 2 tablespoons light cream or evaporated milk. Mix until the cheese becomes soft and smooth.

3. Wash and dry 4 lettuce leaves and put one on each of the paper plates. Place 2 pear halves, round side up, on each lettuce leaf.

4. With the spatula, carefully spread some of the cream cheese over each of the pear halves, until all the cheese is used up.

5. Wash the sieve and bowl. Dry them. Put the 60 cherries or grapes into the sieve and wash them under cold running water. Shake off all the water. Cut each cherry in half, remove the stem, and take out the pit. If you are using grapes, be sure to remove all the little stems when you cut the grapes in half.

6. Place the cherry or grape halves close to each other, round side up, on the cream cheese. Pass around the French dressing.

Coffee Pudding

(FOR 4 PEOPLE)

You will need:

1 package instant vanilla pudding

1 teaspoon powdered instant coffee

1½ cups milk

¼ cup heavy cream

You will use:

1 big mixing bowl

Measuring spoon

1 mixing spoon

Measuring cup

Rotary beater

1 small mixing bowl

Wax paper

4 dessert bowls

Prepare it this way:

1. Open the package of instant vanilla pudding and put the pudding powder into the big mixing bowl. Add 1 teaspoon instant coffee to the pudding powder in the bowl and mix.

2. Measure 1½ cups milk. Add a little to the pudding and beat with the rotary beater. Add a little more and beat again. Do this until you have used all the milk. By then the pudding will be smooth and creamy.

3. Measure ¼ cup heavy cream and pour it into the small mixing bowl. Wash and dry the rotary beater. When it is clean, whip the cream with it, until the cream is nice and stiff. With wax paper, cover both bowls—the one with the pudding and the one with the whipped cream—and put them into the refrigerator for exactly 1 hour.

4. Just before serving, put the pudding into the bowls and top each serving with a little of the whipped cream.

Chocolate Frosted Angel Cake

(FOR 8 PEOPLE)

You will need:

2 3-ounce packages cream cheese

1 teaspoon milk

2½ cups confectioners' sugar

1 tablespoon chocolate syrup

1 teaspoon vanilla

⅛ teaspoon salt

1 8-inch unfrosted angel food cake

You will use:

Measuring spoons

Mixing bowl

Mixing spoon

Measuring cups

Wax paper, 9 by 9 inches

Spatula

1 9-inch paper doily

Cake platter

Scissors

8 small paper plates

Prepare it this way:

1. Put the cream cheese into the mixing bowl. Add 1 teaspoon milk and blend it into the cream cheese with the spoon.

2. Gradually add the 2½ cups confectioners' sugar and mix until the cheese and the sugar are well blended.

3. Add 1 tablespoon chocolate syrup, 1 teaspoon vanilla, and ⅛ teaspoon salt. Stir again until everything is well mixed.

4. Put the angel food cake on the piece of wax paper. With the spatula, put the cream cheese mixture smoothly over the cake, covering the top and sides. When the cake is all covered, put the paper doily on the cake platter. Lift the cake very carefully with the wax paper and put it on the platter. With the scissors, cut off the wax paper around the cake.

5. Put the cake into the refrigerator for at least 3 hours, and then invite your friends over to eat it. They will like it.

Cranberry Whip

(FOR 4 PEOPLE)

You will need:

2 eggs

1 tablespoon milk or water

1 16-ounce can (2 cups) whole cranberry sauce

4 tablespoons chopped walnuts

You will use:

2 teacups or small bowls

Mixing bowl

1 small plate or aluminum foil

Rotary beater

Can opener

Mixing spoon

Measuring spoon

1 large plate or aluminum foil

4 dessert bowls

Prepare it this way:

1. Separate the egg whites from the egg yolks this way: Crack 1 egg by tapping it gently against the edge of a teacup or small bowl. Hold the cracked egg over the cup or bowl and let the white drip into it. When all the white has dripped into the cup, put the egg yolk into another cup or bowl. Put the white into the mixing bowl. Crack the other egg over the cup and add the white to the first one. Put the second yolk into the cup or bowl with the first yolk. Put 1 tablespoon milk (or

water) over the egg yolks so they won't dry out. Cover the cup or bowl with a small plate or aluminum foil, and store in the refrigerator. You will not need the yolks in this recipe, but your mother will be able to use them in cooking.

2. Beat the 2 egg whites with the rotary beater until they are stiff and stand in peaks.

3. Open the can of whole cranberry sauce and fold the cranberry sauce into the egg whites this way: With the mixing spoon, place some of the cranberry sauce on top of the egg whites in the bowl and gently lift some of the egg white from the bottom of the bowl over the cranberry sauce. Repeat until the cranberry sauce is mixed into the egg whites. Then add some more cranberry sauce and fold it in the same way. Keep doing this until you have added all the cranberry sauce.

4. Add 4 tablespoons chopped walnuts and mix them lightly with the cranberry and egg white mixture.

5. Cover the mixing bowl with a large plate or aluminum foil and chill in the refrigerator for at least 2 hours. Then serve it in your dessert bowls.

Applesauce with Sour Cream

(FOR 4 PEOPLE)

You will need:

2 8-ounce jars or cans applesauce	1 tablespoon brown sugar
½ cup sour cream	1 teaspoon diluted frozen lemon juice

You will use:

Can opener	Measuring spoon
1 big mixing bowl	Mixing spoon
Measuring cup	4 dessert bowls

Prepare it this way:

1. Open the jars or cans of applesauce, and put the applesauce into the big mixing bowl.

2. Measure ½ cup sour cream, 1 tablespoon brown sugar, and 1 teaspoon lemon juice. Add these to the bowl with the applesauce. Mix it well with the spoon and put into the refrigerator for at least 1 hour. Then you are ready to serve.

Apricot Pie

(FOR 8 PEOPLE)

You will need:

1 1-pound can apricot halves

12 lemon snaps

¼ cup (⅛ pound) butter

1 tablespoon brown sugar

1 package instant vanilla pudding

1¼ cups milk

You will use:

Can opener

Sieve

1 large bowl to use with the sieve

Clean dish towel

Wooden mallet or small hammer

1 small mixing bowl

Measuring cups

9-inch pie pan

Measuring spoon

1 large mixing bowl

Rotary beater

Wax paper

8 dessert plates

44

Prepare it this way:

1. Open the can of apricot halves and put the apricots into the sieve over the large bowl. Drain off all the syrup.

2. Crush the lemon snaps into tiny pieces and crumbs. Here is an easy way to do this: Place the snaps on one half of a clean dish towel. Fold the other half of the towel over the snaps. Pound gently with a wooden mallet or small hammer until all the snaps are crushed. You should have about 1 cup of crumbs. Put them into the small mixing bowl.

3. Put ¼ cup butter into a cup. Place the cup in a bowl of hot water from the tap. Be sure the water does not get into the cup with the butter.

4. When the butter is soft, add it to the cracker crumbs and mix well.

5. Press the mixture of crumbs and butter into the pie pan, covering the bottom and sides of the pan.

6. Put the apricot halves, round side up, on top of the cracker crust. The number of apricots you will have will just about cover the bottom of the pie pan. Sprinkle the apricots with 1 tablespoon brown sugar.

7. Open the package of vanilla pudding and put the pudding powder into a large mixing bowl. Slowly add 1¼ cups milk, mixing the pudding powder and the milk with the rotary beater until the pudding is smooth.

8. Pour the pudding over the apricots in the pie pan and cover with wax paper. Put into the refrigerator to chill for 3 hours. Then it will be just right for eating.

Ice Cream Pie

(FOR 8 PEOPLE)

You will need:

12 graham crackers

1 tablespoon sugar

¼ cup (⅛ pound) butter

1 package strawberry gelatin

1 cup hot water from the tap

1 pint strawberry ice cream

½ cup heavy cream

1 tablespoon confectioners' sugar

You will use:

Measuring cup

Measuring spoons

2 mixing bowls

1 mixing spoon

8-inch pie pan

Rotary beater

Aluminum foil

8 paper plates

Prepare it this way:

1. Melt the butter by putting the cup with the butter into a bowl of hot water from the tap.

2. With your hands, crush the graham crackers into tiny pieces and crumbs. You should have about 1 cup of crumbs.

3. Put the crushed graham crackers and the 1 tablespoon sugar into one of the mixing bowls.

4. Add the melted butter to the crackers. Mix together.

5. Line the bottom and sides of the 8-inch pie pan with the cracker and butter mixture.

6. Open the package of strawberry gelatin and put the gelatin powder into the other mixing bowl. Add 1 cup hot water from the tap. Stir until the gelatin dissolves. When the gelatin has melted, add 1 pint strawberry ice cream to it and stir until the ice cream has also melted. Let the mixture stand for 5 minutes. Then beat the ice cream and

gelatin mixture with the rotary beater for about 5 minutes, so that it becomes light and fluffy.

7. Pour the gelatin and ice cream mixture into the pie pan lined with the graham crackers. Cover with aluminum foil and put into the refrigerator for at least 4 hours before serving.

8. Just before serving, whip ½ cup heavy cream with 1 tablespoon confectioners' sugar until the cream is stiff. Put the whipped cream on the pie and serve immediately. Don't forget to invite company; the pie will be enough for eight people.

Chocolate Banana Pudding

(FOR 4 PEOPLE)

You will need:

1 large very ripe banana	1¼ cups milk
1 package instant chocolate pudding	½ cup heavy cream

You will use:

2 big bowls	1 big spoon
1 fork	1 large plate
Measuring cup	4 dessert bowls
Rotary beater	

Prepare it this way:

1. Peel the banana and place it in one of the big bowls. Mash the banana well with the fork, until it is almost watery.

2. Open the package of pudding and add the pudding powder to the banana in the bowl.

3. Measure 1¼ cups milk and add it slowly to the mixture. Mix with the rotary beater until smooth.

4. Wash and dry the rotary beater. Whip the cream in the other bowl until it is very stiff.

5. Add the whipped cream to the chocolate pudding and mix together. Cover the bowl with a plate and place it in the refrigerator for at least 1 hour.

6. When you are ready to serve, put the pudding into dessert bowls and eat it right away.

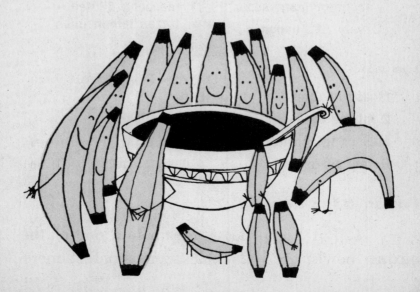

Banana-Prune Whip

(FOR 4 PEOPLE)

You will need:

½ cup heavy cream

2 tablespoons confectioners' sugar

2 very ripe bananas

1 cup baby food strained prunes

1 teaspoon diluted frozen lemon juice

You will use:

Measuring cup

2 mixing bowls

Measuring spoons

Rotary beater

Fork

Mixing spoon

1 large plate

4 dessert bowls

Prepare it this way:

1. Put ½ cup heavy cream into one of the mixing bowls. Add 2 tablespoons confectioners'

52

sugar to the cream, and beat it with the rotary beater until stiff.

2. Peel the bananas and put them in the other bowl. Mash them with the fork. The bananas should be almost watery when you finish mashing them. Add to the mashed bananas 1 cup baby food strained prunes and 1 teaspoon lemon juice. Mix well with the spoon.

3. Add the whipped cream to the bananas and prunes and mix them together.

4. Cover the bowl with the plate and put it into the refrigerator for 1 hour. Then serve at once in your dessert bowls.

Eggnog with Doughnuts

You will need:

6 eggs

12 tablespoons (¾ cup) sugar

3 teaspoons vanilla

1 teaspoon salt

12 cups (3 quarts) milk

3 teaspoons cinnamon

12 doughnuts

1 cup confectioners' sugar

You will use:

1 teacup or small bowl

1 very large mixing bowl

1 glass jar with a cover

Measuring spoons

Mixing spoon

Measuring cup

1 large plate or aluminum foil

Punch bowl

Ladle or big spoon

12 cups

Prepare the eggnog this way:

1. Separate the egg yolks from the egg whites. To do this, crack 1 egg over a teacup or small bowl and let the white drip into it. Put the yolk in the big mixing bowl and put the egg white into the glass jar. Crack another egg over the cup and let the white drip into it. Add the egg yolk to the first one in the mixing bowl and put the egg white into the jar. Do this until you have separated all 6 eggs and have all the yolks in the mixing bowl. (Keep out 1 egg white to use in the Chocolate Marshmallow Candy.) Put the cover on the jar containing the rest of the egg whites and put it in the refrigerator. The whites can be used the next day by your mother.

2. Gradually add 12 tablespoons sugar to the egg yolks, mixing them together as you add the sugar. Mix until everything is smooth and the sugar has almost dissolved.

3. Add to the yolks and sugar mixture 3 teaspoons vanilla and 1 teaspoon salt. Mix well again.

4. Little by little, add 12 cups milk, stirring the egg yolk mixture as you pour in the milk. When the egg yolks, sugar, vanilla, and salt are all well mixed with the milk, cover the bowl with a large plate or aluminum foil and put it into the refrigerator for at least 2 hours.

5. Pour the eggnog from the mixing bowl into your prettiest punch bowl or serving bowl and sprinkle it with 3 teaspoons cinnamon. Serve with the ladle or a big spoon into cups.

With the eggnog, serve doughnuts. Buy plain doughnuts in your bakery or grocery store and sprinkle them with confectioners' sugar.

Chocolate Marshmallow Candy

You will need:

1 package instant chocolate nut pudding

1 pound confectioners' sugar

1 egg white

2 tablespoons milk or cream

⅓ cup butter

⅓ cup prepared marshmallow cream

You will use:

1 large mixing bowl

Measuring spoon

Mixing spoon

Measuring cup

Large piece of wax paper

Bread board

Rolling pin

Knife

Large candy dish or platter

Paper doily to fit over the candy dish or platter

58

Prepare it this way:

1. Open the package of instant chocolate nut pudding and put the pudding powder into the mixing bowl. Add to it 1 pound confectioners sugar.

2. Pour over the sugar and pudding 2 tablespoons milk or cream. Add 1 egg white. (Use the egg white you kept out when you made the eggnog, or see page 77 for directions on separating eggs.) Mix the sugar and the pudding with the milk and egg white.

3. Measure ⅓ cup butter and put the cup with the butter into a bowl of warm water from the tap. Let the butter melt a little. Don't melt it entirely; just soften it up a bit.

4. Add the softened butter to the bowl with the pudding and sugar mixture. Mix it with the spoon for about 3 minutes. Then wash your hands very, very well and dry them. Using your hands, knead (mix) the pudding and sugar mixture until it becomes like a dough. It should take you about 3 or 4 minutes to do this.

5. Put the large piece of wax paper on the bread board. Sprinkle a little confectioners' sugar on the wax paper and put the candy dough on the wax paper. With the rolling pin, roll out the candy dough until it is about ¼ inch thick. Try to roll it into a square shape, not a round shape. Cut the candy dough into 5 strips, each 1½ inches wide.

6. Spread 4 of the strips with marshmallow cream (it comes in jars), and pile them one on top of the other. Do not spread the fifth strip. Put it on top. Wrap the candy in the wax paper on which it was rolled and put it into the refrigerator for at least 3 hours. Handle the candy very carefully when you are putting it into the refrigerator so that you do not break it.

7. When the candy has hardened, take it out of the refrigerator and put it back on the bread board. Open the wax paper wrapping. Cut the candy strip into ¼-inch slices. Have the candy dish or platter handy and put the paper doily on it. As you cut the candy, put it on the doily and you are all ready. It's fun to prepare and it certainly tastes good.

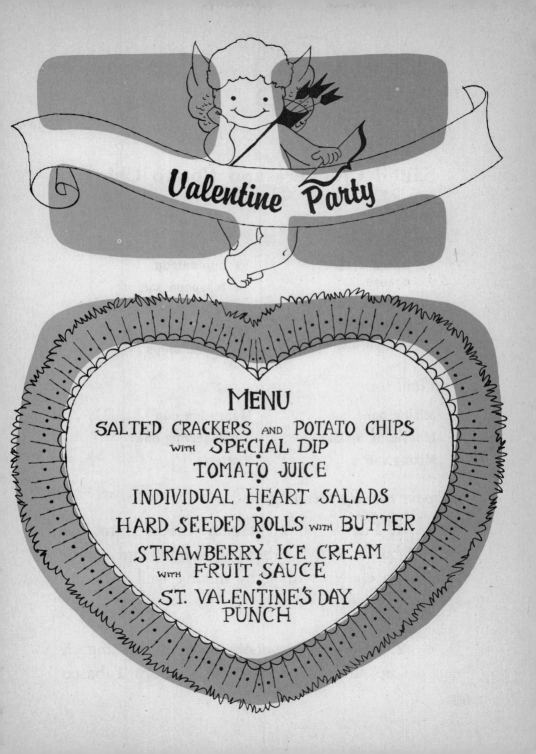

Valentine Party

MENU
SALTED CRACKERS AND POTATO CHIPS
WITH SPECIAL DIP

TOMATO JUICE

INDIVIDUAL HEART SALADS

HARD SEEDED ROLLS WITH BUTTER

STRAWBERRY ICE CREAM
WITH FRUIT SAUCE

ST. VALENTINE'S DAY
PUNCH

Salted Crackers and Potato Chips with Special Dip

You will need:

½ pound cream cheese

2 tablespoons milk

2 tablespoons French dressing

⅓ cup catsup

¼ teaspoon salt

4 drops Tabasco sauce

Salted crackers and potato chips

You will use:

Mixing bowl

Measuring spoons

Mixing spoon

Measuring cup

Small serving bowl

Platter

Prepare the dip this way:

1. Put ½ pound cream cheese into the mixing bowl. Add 2 tablespoons milk and soften the cream cheese with it by mixing well with the spoon.

2. Add 2 tablespoons French dressing, ⅓ cup catsup, and ¼ teaspoon salt, 4 drops Tabasco sauce. (Be sure that you do not use more than 4 drops Tabasco sauce. It is very hot.) Mix all these things well with the cheese.

3. Put the cheese mixture into your serving bowl and set the bowl in the center of the platter. Put the potato chips and crackers on the platter, all around the bowl. Serve with the tomato juice. Everyone will dip the crackers and potato chips into the cheese mixture and eat them while they have the tomato juice.

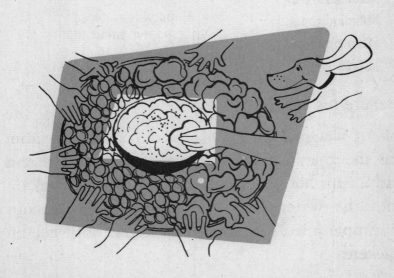

Individual Heart Salads

You will need:

2 packages raspberry gelatin

2 cups hot water from the tap

1½ cups pineapple juice

2 cups crushed pineapple

8 lettuce leaves

Ready-made French dressing

16 hard seeded rolls

½ pound butter

You will use:

Mixing bowl

Measuring cup

Mixing spoon

Can opener

Sieve

Large bowl to use with the sieve

8 individual heart-shaped salad molds

8 salad plates

Prepare the salads this way:

1. Open the 2 packages of raspberry gelatin. Put the gelatin powder into the mixing bowl and add 2 cups hot water from the tap. Mix the gelatin with the water until it dissolves. Add 1½ cups pineapple juice. Let stand 5 minutes, until gelatin thickens.

2. Open a large can of crushed pineapple. Put the pineapple into the sieve over the large bowl and drain it well. Measure 2 cups drained crushed pineapple and add it to the thickened gelatin. Mix well. Pour the gelatin and pineapple mixture into the 8 individual salad molds and put them into the refrigerator for at least 4 hours.

3. Wash and dry the lettuce leaves and put one on each salad plate. Unmold the salads by dipping each mold into a bowl of warm water so that the water covers the bottom and comes halfway up the sides of the mold. Keep the mold in the warm water for 1 minute—no longer—and then turn it over on top of the lettuce leaf.

4. Put a bottle of ready-made French dressing on the table so everyone can help himself.

5. Serve with hard seeded rolls and butter. Buy about 16 rolls and ½ pound (2 sticks) butter.

St. Valentine's Day Punch

You will need:

12 ice cubes

2 cups chilled grape juice

1 quart (4 cups) chilled orange juice

2 quarts (8 cups) ginger ale

¼ cup sugar

2 oranges

You will use:

Punch bowl or other very large bowl

Measuring cup

Mixing spoon

Knife

Ladle

8 punch cups or glasses

Prepare it this way:

1. Put 12 ice cubes in the punch bowl. Pour over them 2 cups chilled grape juice, 1 quart chilled orange juice, and 2 quarts ginger ale. Add ¼ cup sugar and mix it all very well.

2. Peel and slice 2 oranges. Remove all seeds. Float the orange slices in the punch bowl. Serve with a ladle into the punch cups or glasses.

Strawberry Ice Cream
with Fruit Sauce

You will need:

2 packages frozen
strawberries

2 pints strawberry ice
cream

You will use:

Mixing bowl

8 dessert bowls

Prepare it this way:

1. Open the 2 packages of frozen strawberries and put them into the mixing bowl. Let stand until they are defrosted, about 45 minutes or 1 hour.

2. Divide the 2 pints ice cream into 8 portions and place 1 portion in each of the dessert bowls.

3. Pour over each portion of ice cream a little of the frozen strawberries and the syrup they come in.

Mother's Day Party

MENU

Cheddar Cheese Salad Bowl

Rye Bread with Butter

Baked Apples
in
Vanilla Cream

Cheddar Cheese Salad Bowl

You will need:

2 heads lettuce	⅓ cup ready-made French dressing
4 very firm tomatoes	2 loaves rye bread
2 cucumbers	½ pound (2 sticks) butter
14 radishes	
12 slices of Cheddar cheese	

You will use:

Paper towels	Salad fork and spoon
Knife	8 paper plates
Sieve	Bread basket
Large salad bowl	Butter dish
Measuring cup	

Prepare it this way:

1. Wash all the vegetables in cold water. With paper towels, dry the lettuce, tomatoes, cucumbers, and radishes.

2. Cut the tops and tails from the radishes.

3. Tear the lettuce into bite-sized pieces and put them into the salad bowl.

4. Slice the cucumbers. Do not peel them, and make the slices quite thick. Put the slices in the salad bowl on top of the lettuce.

5. Cut the tomatoes into wedges and add them to the salad bowl.

6. Slice the radishes thin and add them to the salad bowl, too.

7. Cut the Cheddar cheese slices into thin strips and add them to the salad. (You can buy packaged sliced Cheddar cheese.)

8. Measure ⅓ cup ready-made French dressing and pour it over the salad. With the salad fork and spoon, toss the salad lightly until everything is well mixed. Serve in the salad bowl and let the guests help themselves.

9. Unwrap the loaves of rye bread and place the slices in a bread basket. This bread will be very good with the salad.

Baked Apples in Vanilla Sauce

You will need:

2 cans baked apples

1 package instant vanilla pudding

2½ cups milk

8 maraschino cherries

You will use:

Can opener

1 large bowl to use with the sieve

8 large dessert or cereal bowls

Mixing bowl

Mixing spoon

Measuring cup

Prepare it this way:

1. Open the cans of baked apples. There are 4 apples in each can. Put the apples into the sieve and drain them well over the large bowl. Put 1 apple into each of the 8 serving bowls.

2. Open the package of instant vanilla pudding. Put the pudding powder into the mixing bowl. Add 2½ cups milk very slowly, mixing the pudding all the time, until you have added all the milk and the pudding is nice and smooth.

3. Pour a little of the pudding sauce over each apple. You will have enough to almost cover the apples. Put the bowls with the apples and sauce into the refrigerator for at least 2 hours. Just before serving, place a maraschino cherry on top of each apple.

Halloween Party

MENU
Apple Cider
Black and White Sandwiches
Polished Red Apples.
Butterscotch and Peanut Butter
Candy

Black and White Sandwiches

You will need:

12 slices white bread

12 slices pumpernickel or whole wheat bread

1 pound ready-made Cheddar cheese spread

½ pound ready-made deviled ham spread

You will use:

Bread board

Spreading knife

Wax paper

Cutting knife

Paper doily

Platter

Prepare them this way:

1. Make 3 separate stacks of bread. Each stack should have 3 slices of white bread and 3 slices of black pumpernickel or whole wheat bread.

2. Take the first stack and spread 2 slices of pumpernickel or whole wheat bread with Cheddar cheese spread. Spread 3 slices of white bread with deviled ham spread. On top of a piece of dark bread with Cheddar cheese, put a piece of white bread with deviled ham. Then on top of the white bread put a piece of dark bread with cheese, then another piece of white bread with ham, and top it with the unspread slice of dark bread. Press the stack together with your hands and wrap it in a piece of wax paper. Put it into the refrigerator for at least 3 hours.

3. Do the other 2 stacks of bread in exactly the same way and put them into the refrigerator with the first one.

4. After all 3 stacks have been chilled in the refrigerator for 3 hours, take them out and cut each stack lengthwise into ½-inch slices. Then cut each slice into 3 strips. The sandwiches will look like ribbons and be very pretty. They'll taste good, too.

Butterscotch and Peanut Butter Candy

You will need:

1 package instant butterscotch pudding

1 pound confectioners' sugar

1 egg white

2 tablespoons milk or cream

1 tablespoon cold water or milk

⅓ cup butter

½ cup creamy peanut butter

You will use:

1 large mixing bowl

1 teacup or small bowl

1 small glass jar with a cover

Measuring spoon

Mixing spoon

Measuring cup

Large piece of wax paper

Bread board

Rolling pin

Knife

Large candy dish or platter

Paper doily to fit over the candy dish or platter

Prepare it this way:

1. Open the package of instant butterscotch pudding and put the pudding powder into the mixing bowl. Add to it 1 pound confectioners' sugar and 2 tablespoons milk or cream.

2. Separate the egg this way: Crack the egg over the teacup or small bowl and let the white drip into it. Put the egg yolk into the small jar and cover it with 1 tablespoon cold water or milk to keep it from drying out. Put the cover on the jar and put it into the refrigerator. (You will not need the yolk to make this candy, but your mother can use it in cooking.) Put the egg white into the large mixing bowl, with the pudding powder, confectioners' sugar, and milk or cream. Mix them well.

3. Measure ⅓ cup butter and put the cup with the butter into a bowl of warm water from the tap. Be sure the water does not get into the cup with the butter. Let the butter melt a little. Don't melt it entirely; just soften it up a bit.

4. Add the softened butter to the bowl with the pudding and sugar mixture. Mix it with the spoon for about 3 minutes. Then wash your hands very well and dry them. Using your hands, knead (mix) the pudding and sugar mixture until it becomes like a dough. This should take you about 3 or 4 minutes.

5. Put the large piece of wax paper on the bread board. Sprinkle a little confectioners' sugar on the wax paper and put the candy dough on the wax paper. With the rolling pin, roll out the candy dough until it is about ¼ inch thick. Try to roll it into a square shape, not a round shape. Cut the dough into 5 strips, each 1½ inches wide.

6. Spread four of the strips with creamy peanut butter and pile them on top of one another. Do not spread the fifth strip. Put it on top. Wrap the candy in the wax paper on which it was rolled and put it into the refrigerator for at least 3 hours. Handle the candy very carefully when you are putting it into the refrigerator so that you do not break it.

7. When the candy has hardened, take it out of the refrigerator and put it back on the bread board. Open the wax paper wrapping. Cut the candy strip into ¼-inch slices. Have the candy dish or platter handy and put the paper doily on it. As you cut the candy, put it on the doily and you are all ready. This is fun to make and very good to eat.

INDEX